Caught in the Crosshairs of War

Special Edition
November 24, 2024, Page 56-58

Gale Nemec

Illustrations
John Fristoe Sr.

Photography
Nemec Family & Friends

Front Cover
Sharing is Caring eBook covers by Dawn LeGros

This book was completed with help from these wonderful people. Thank you.

Patrick Gallagher
Lorrie Fox Semonian
Shirley Sprinkle
Special Edition Debbie Nemec

All rights reserved. No part of this book may be reproduced in any form or by electronic means, video, digital or mechanical, including information storage and retrieval systems, without written permission from the publisher, except for brief passages quoted in reviews.

ISBN 978-1-947608-09-2
Nemec Productions LLC
Alexandria, Virginia

Copyright © 2019,2020,2021,2022,2023,2024,2025

Gale B. Nemec

DEDICATION

To those in America's armed forces and the 1968 International Archeology Convention in Czechoslovakia. To James Nemec's determination and his bravery. To his supportive, trusting wife, Ruth Nemec, and to their calm, positive attitudes. To Ruthie Nemec, who made it through from afar. To Miracle and to "Miracles." To America the Beautiful, its magnificent stars, and stripes and what it represents.

To my immediate and extended family so they will know this event is part of their heritage.

DEDICATED TO *YOU*
THANK YOU FOR BUYING MY BOOK

This personal account of *Prague Spring* is important to everyone's life and reminds us how easily freedom can be taken from us. Please buy this book for families, schools, book clubs and as a gift for any occasion. I would appreciate it if you would rate this non-fiction book on *Good Reads, Amazon, Facebook* and where you bought it with a star value or a review. Thank you!

ACKNOWLEDGMENTS

Faith, unconditional love, education, and travel are some of the greatest gifts parents can give their children. These gifts can never be taken away. A combination of these gifts from my parents gave me a full appreciation for God/Jesus the United States of America and its place in the world.

SPECIAL THANKS

Debbie Nemec

Joy Loper

Jane Gallagher

Justin Mohay

Dorrie Robinson

PREFACE

There are nine eyewitness accounts to this life-altering event that changed our family forever. This one account is based on my memories and notes.

It was updated on August 21, 2023, to include Debbie's, Joy's and Francies memories.

It was updated again on November 24, 2024, to include a new photo and Debbie's and Ruthies memories relating to the event surrounding the photo.

This book replaces the first and second *Caught in the Crosshairs of War* books. This book will be an updated book as we find notes and photographs related to this event. The next update will be *Ruthies Experience from home.*

Note: Family members' names may have been changed.

This book belongs to

_____

This book is from

_____

Today's date

_____

Charles Bridge. Prague, Czechoslovakia
Copyright 2018-2025 All Rights Reserved

CHAPTER ONE

From early childhood, on the Fourth of July - Independence Day and other patriotic holidays, Mom and Dad would have us take turns raising the American flag, on the huge flagpole in our front yard, and would lead us in the Pledge of Allegiance and patriotic songs. All nine of us, and sometimes with friends, would sing *The Star-Spangled Banner, America the Beautiful, My Country 'tis of Thee* and other patriotic songs.

It was exciting! Early on, I learned it was important to understand and respect our nation, its flag, and our national holidays, and to know, say and believe in the Pledge of Allegiance.

At first, I loved this tradition. I could not wait to run outside, raise, and salute our flag and sing patriotic songs with their wonderful rhythms, harmony, and lyrics. It was so much fun to sing, and we all loved to sing in harmony.

I was thrilled when it was my turn to attach the flag grommets to the pole clips and pull the ropes that took the American flag to the top of the flagpole. With broad smiles and our hands on our hearts, we would all proudly watch as our American flag waved in the breeze. We knew it meant so much.

But when I reached my teens, when national holidays arrived, I complained. I did not want to raise the flag, say the pledge or sing. I wanted to watch TV, hang out with my friends, or talk on the phone. Then something happened that changed my life forever.

CHAPTER TWO

August 1968. Our family was touring through Europe. There were seven children: Mary, Ruthie, Francie, Gale, Jimmy, Debbie, and Joy. We ranged from under ten years of age to the early twenties. Mom and Dad, in our minds, were ageless. Dad, a hard-working visionary, had been a Commander in the Navy before starting his own business. Mom ran the household, the community, our homerooms, and, unbeknownst to her, was the marketing genius for Dad's business.

We traveled through Europe in a blue and white, Volkswagen bus, which we nick-named the *Truckey Bus*. As you can imagine, with a large family we had a lot of luggage and, to keep it all straight, we used white paint to paint our initials on our suitcases. We took the tube of paint with us on the trip in case we bought more luggage.

Dad figured Debbie was strong and light enough to stand on the top of the bus and organize our luggage so we would have room to sit inside the Truckey Bus. Debbie and Francie came up with a pattern for the luggage and Francie drew it on the back of a luggage tag. Each suitcase, in its own shape and size, fit in its place on the roof of the bus.

Every morning Debbie would stand on top of the bus, as Francie, reading the chart, would hand the correct suitcase to Ruthie, or another sibling, who would hand it up to Debbie. Debbie would fit the suitcase into the pattern so that not an inch of space was wasted. When all the suitcases were in place, Debbie would jump off the top of the bus and we would drive to our next destination.

Early in our trip, Jimmy started telling a joke with the punch line, "Does anybody have an apple?" He told the joke so much that we'd roll our eyes and kind of laugh or say, "Jimmy!! Not again!" Or "Ha, ha. Never heard that before."

A big part of this trip to Europe was a visit to Czechoslovakia, the country of my father's family.

August 18, 1968. Ruthie returned to the United States to prepare for her new job as an elementary school teacher. After taking her to the airport, the eight of us continued our travel. We were heading for Czechoslovakia and passed several armored tanks along the road. It was odd.

August 19, 1968. We entered Czechoslovakia, which had become a communist nation under Russian rule. At the border crossing, we were told that by law we were allowed to be in the country for two nights and were required, without question, to leave the country on day three or face dire consequences. We had exactly two and a half days to see Czechoslovakia, discover its history and visit its capital city, Prague.

It was rainy and overcast when we crossed the Czechoslovakian border. Upon driving through the raised gate, the poorly paved road became a dirt, rocky road. There was a thick, deep-green forest to our right and a muddy field with trees to our left. Surprisingly, we saw more armored tanks and armed soldiers with rifles who directed us to the side of the road.

At one point they commanded us to stop and get out of our Truckey Bus while they drove the tanks into the forest. They told Dad to drive the bus to the other side of the field. They told the rest of us to walk through the field and join Dad on the other side. These same commands were given to anyone crossing the border in a car. It was so strange! We did not know why we were commanded to comply with these instructions, but we followed the soldiers' orders.

There was an eerie feeling as we walked across the field and watched the soldiers maneuver the roaring tanks deep into the forest. After what seemed like forever, we caught up with Dad and got into the Truckey Bus.

The soldiers waved us on and allowed us to continue our trip through Czechoslovakia. We did not know what was taking place, but it looked like the military was practicing their maneuvers and nothing more.

Arriving in Prague, we quickly discovered that all the hotels were full because the city was hosting an international convention of archeologists. Dad could not find a place for eight of us to stay, but, in typical Dad fashion, he spoke to everyone he saw on the street and, through one of his encounters, he met a man whose sister had a large two-room apartment off Wenceslas Square. It was perfect! Finding the apartment to rent for two nights was a miracle for us, so we nicknamed the man "Miracle."

Unpacking the Truckey Bus, we climbed the dark stairwell ending at an outdoor corridor which led to the apartment on the third floor. The apartment had lots of windows and sunlight, and its building shaped the back of a cobblestone square courtyard. It was next to the Telegraph office building. It was exciting!

We could look out of the large, screenless windows and watch people walk or drive their cars through the courtyard and under an archway as they cut between a side street and the main road in Wencelas Square. The two-room apartment had a couch, three large beds, which we shared, and a bathroom down the hall. It would be our family's cozy home for the next two days. It was exactly what we needed, and we loved it.

Czechoslovakia was Dad's ancestral home. We had heard about it our whole lives, which made it more fascinating. Dad had spoken the Czech language until the age of six when he entered public school where he learned the English language. While in Czechoslovakia, he began to pick up bits and pieces of the language he learned in his early childhood.

It was a beautiful day and most of us were outside with Dad while Mom and Joy were in the apartment enjoying an intimate mother - daughter conversation. The windows were open, and rays of sunlight were pouring in. Mom decided to open her bible and read John 3:16 to Joy. *"For God so loved the world that He gave his only begotten son. That whosoever believes in Him should not perish but have everlasting life.*

After mom read the verse she said, "Joy, do you believe that Jesus came and died for our sins?"

Joy said, "Yes. I do believe that" and Mom hugged Joy.

Peace filled the room, and it was flooded with more sunlight. There was no darkness and calmness for both mom and Joy. Mom had tears in her eyes knowing that her youngest child would go to heaven with the rest of us if something happened.

Our first night, Miracle took us to a restaurant where he knew we could get a traditional Czech meal. A meal that we all loved and enjoyed every Christmas. Early in Mom's and Dad's marriage Mom learned to make the meal from Dad's mother. It consisted of chicken noodle soup, duck, dumplings, sauerkraut, cucumber vinegar salad and Listy for dessert. Listy, the Czech word for leaves, is rolled-out dough, dried, sliced, and fried with lots of powdered sugar and it takes two days to make. I learned to make it and made it at Christmas. We all loved Listy.

Miracle spoke in whispers as he described the bubbling undercurrent of the Czechoslovakian people. Their Communists party leader, Alexander Dubček, was granting the country the long-denied gifts of freedom, a little at a time, and, so far, Russia was allowing it to happen. A few of the new freedoms included freedom of speech, the end of censorship and allowing the public to criticize the government. Dubček said he was creating "socialism with a human face" and the "democratization" of the country. The world could not believe what was happening in the communist controlled nation and watched in quiet, hopeful anticipation.

Dad had spoken to us about this at length, and now we were hearing about it firsthand. It was fascinating, and we all shared Miracle's enthusiasm but dared not speak loudly so as not to be overheard.
During the day we saw the streetlights were on. Debbie asked our host why. Miracle told us the Czech people were forced to pay Russia for electricity. Therefore, the country was required to leave the streetlights on twenty-four hours a day.

Miracle also told us that cars were a luxury, difficult to get and nearly impossible to repair. People saved for years and years to buy or pay for the repair of a car.

Another thing we asked about was the construction of the unfinished buildings we saw when we entered the country. Miracle told us if we looked closely, we would see the beams were rusted out. The buildings were for "show" by the Russians to indicate to foreigners, from a distance, that there was growth in Czechoslovakia, a communist nation. Where in reality there was none.

These were surprising revelations which showed us just a few of the aspects of what it was like to live in a communist nation and under Russian rule. Miracle also pointed out that the huge speakers mounted on the buildings was how Russian leadership communicated with the Czech people.

The evening was wonderful and filled with deep conversation, good food, sights, insights, and a breathtakingly beautiful walk home. The sky was clear, the temperature was perfect and white lights decorated a few of the historic fences. We were fully experiencing the old and genteel world of Czechoslovakia.

Back at our apartment we fell asleep — happy to be in the land of our ancestors and sad that we had to leave the country in two days. There was so much to see, a fleeting time to see it, and we hadn't scratched the surface.

In the middle of the night, as we all slept, Czechoslovakia changed drastically . . . against her will . . . and our lives changed forever.

CHAPTER THREE

August 21,1968. I woke up early. From my bed I saw Dad standing by the window and looking up at the sky. He was not smiling, and his gaze was steady, serious, and solemn. The room was strangely silent. I said, "Good Morning, Dad!"

He saw that I was awake, put his finger to his lips and motioned for me to be quiet. He pointed to the hazy sky and whispered, "Listen. Transport planes."

Wide awake I whispered, "From where, why?"

"Not sure," he whispered, "I think Czechoslovakia has been invaded."

I knew transport planes, were military planes, filled with armed soldiers and equipment, and now they were flying overhead. From our bed, I could hear the planes. Carefully, I crawled over my sleeping sisters and brother and joined Dad at the screenless window. There was a surreal feeling in the air as we watched the planes fly over Prague to land at some unknown destination. I felt so close to the country of my father's heritage, and I'd only been there a few hours. Not so slowly, the rest of the family woke up and spoke in whispered tones trying to comprehend the situation we now found ourselves in.

Mom quietly said the night before, when she and Debbie went down the hall to use the bathroom, they saw and heard, '. . . a man speaking with his sister as they walked toward us. Talking in

Czechoslovakian, she thought they said Czechoslovakia had been invaded by Russia, and several other countries.'

Mom also told us when she had gotten back in bed and told Dad she thought Czechoslovakia had been invaded, in his sleep filled mind he said, "You're dreaming. You don't know Czech. Go back to sleep."

When she told us what she had learned the night before, like Dad, we didn't believe her. She didn't speak the Czech language. But, when we began to hear the erratic sounds of gunfire, the muffled sounds of crowds yelling in unison, and seeing people running through the courtyard signaled to us something dangerous had occurred. One by one we came to realize that Mom was right. Czechoslovakia had been invaded!

Stunned and speechless, we instantly went from touring the beautiful old city to being caught in the crosshairs of war!

Before we had a chance to protest, Dad was dressed, out of our two-room apartment, down the stairs, briskly walking through the square and into the streets to find news and a way to get us home. I remember shouting, "I love you Daddy, be careful," but don't know if he heard me. He waved, however, and disappeared under the archway leading into Wencelas Square.

He couldn't have been gone long but it felt like days. We were left to stare at each other and make ourselves laugh, talk, whisper, and play card games to replace our fears. We didn't want to frighten the younger kids.

When Dad returned, he knew the truth, what had happened and what was happening. He had tears in his eyes.

Having raised us to face just about anything he leveled with us and told us Czechoslovakia had been invaded. There were tanks and soldiers lining every inch of the streets. All the parked cars had been rolled over by the tanks as the tanks drove in and invaded Prague. Nothing had stopped them from their assault.

The invasion had left the Czech people defenseless and in a state of shock. Their armed services had been stripped of their weapons and put under State arrest. The television, radio, telegraph, telephone, and newspapers had been taken over or destroyed in the early hours of the aggression. Propaganda blared from loudspeakers and stated "We've come to protect you. Cooperate with us! We are your friends."

Laws prohibiting the private ownership of firearms solved the Russian governments problem of any individuals banning together or attempting to defend their homes and country.

CHAPTER FOUR

For years, Russia, a communist government, ruled Czechoslovakia and completely controlled the country from its capital, Moscow.

In school I learned a communist country is basically divided into two groups, the elite, and the poor. The government tells the people what they can and cannot do, where they will work, the job they will hold, the place they will live, who they will share their residence with, how much money they will make, the education they will receive, what they are allowed to say or believe and more.

Czechoslovakians did not like being controlled by Russia or being a communist country and had slowly begun to change. The Russian government stealthily watched as new freedoms were granted to the Czechoslovakian people by Dubček. Russia did not want the people to have these freedoms — so, to stop this, they invaded.

As the day progressed, we got more information and learned that hundreds of thousands of troops from Russia, Poland, East Germany, Hungary, and Bulgaria, known as the Warsaw Pact, had invaded Czechoslovakia. The Russian military and her allies surrounded the small, landlocked country, drove armored tanks across the border and had hidden in the forest. Under cover of darkness and in a massive show of power and strength, the huge tanks invaded the country, driving in via streets, alleyways and even sidewalks as they seized Czechoslovakia and its capital, Prague.

The tanks had plowed over and crushed everything in their path including cars, bikes, motorbikes, and buses, and flattened them like pancakes!

Buses were pushed aside like small toys. Armored tanks and countless armed soldiers lined the streets of Prague. Gunfire sporadically and periodically filled the air as the people were shot at, wounded, or killed for no reason.

It. Was. Overwhelming.

From our windows, we could see thick, black smoke rising from numerous locations. We soon learned that the smoke was from radio and television stations, telegraph and newspaper offices being blown up or taken over by the invading military. Destroying these ended factual communications to the Czechoslovakian people and the rest of the world.

Later in the afternoon, a few underground newspapers appeared on the streets. I remember seeing young people peddling fast on their bikes, throwing stacks of papers on the ground, and speeding away. We learned these newspapers were created by students and adults secretly working to get factual news to the public. The newspapers did not last long.

All this happened because Alexander Dubček was granting the people freedom. Freedoms that we in America enjoy every day without thinking about them.

Freedoms that are as simple as: talking about any topic, with your friends in public for as long as you want without fear of being reported, imprisoned or punished; owning and reading the Bible; voting as you choose; having and expressing an opinion that differs from the government; choosing your own career path; building your own business; eating what you want with food left over; freedom to contest elections; freedom to own your own home or a fire-arm without registering it with the government; freedom of religion, speech and the press and all the other freedoms that are granted to us in the Bill of Rights and the United States Constitution.

Wenceslas Square. The military were on maneuvers in Czechoslovakia a few months before the invasion. We learned they thought they were again in the country for maneuvers. They didn't know they were invading the small, landlocked nation.

CHAPTER FIVE

It was our second day in the country. By law we were told when entering the country, we had to leave on the third day or suffer the consequences. But we couldn't leave on the third day. The country had been invaded. We had no idea what to do.

Our American family, with its Czechoslovakian name, was dangerously caught in a war, in the country of our ancestors. We didn't know anyone in the country, we didn't know how to get home, and we were cut off from all outside communication.

It is impossible to imagine what my parents thought or felt during that time. Dad with his loving wife and their kids trapped in an unsuspected war. One child, back in the United States and no way to get in touch with her. Mom with a calm face and doing all she could to take care of us.

We couldn't go out to buy food, and there were no fast-food restaurants. Mom, always thinking ahead, and providing for her family, had purchased Saltines and fruit at local food stands before we had entered the country. Our landlady brought us some tuna fish. Quite frankly, I have no recollection of eating or even thinking of food. It was the last thing on my mind.

That night, a curfew was imposed. Dad wanted us in bed with the lights out when the curfew began. We went to bed not knowing what the morning would bring. We were in a dangerous situation, and Mom and Dad came up with a plan for our safety in the event soldiers burst into the apartment or if gunfire broke out. With great difficulty we all finally fell asleep.

But the horrors of war came to us long before dawn.

August 22,1968. In the middle of the night, we were suddenly awakened by the abrasive sound of gunfire as it cracked through the night air. It sent a message to my sleeping brain that the thousands of troops which had invaded Czechoslovakia the day before were again firing machine guns at whatever was moving.

Instantly, wide awake, I glanced through the windows to see row upon row of thousands of tracer bullets streaking across the ink black sky, just outside of our window, ricocheting off our building and anything in its path.

Francie, legally blind without wearing her glasses, sat up, looked out the window and thought she saw shooting stars. Joy grabbed Francies arm, pulled her away from the window and yelled, "They are shooting at us! Come on! Come on!" as the firing continued.

Immediately our parents' plan shot into action. Mom and Dad yelled, "Kids, Kids! Quick! Grab the mattresses! Grab pillows! Grab blankets! Get in here! Get on the floor! Hurry kids, hurry! Those are tracer bullets!"

With the rapid sound of gunfire ringing in our ears, we grabbed our sisters, brother, pillows, blankets, and mattresses off the beds, and ran as fast as we could into the bedroom.

It was pitch dark. The only light came from the fiery glow of the rows and rows of tracer bullets racing across the sky. The bedroom was the farthest from the front door.

I grabbed my little sister Joy who had tripped, and I yelled, "Come on! Come on!" as I pulled her toward the room with the mattress, only to realize I was pulling her by the arm and standing on her neck at the same time. Instantly, I moved, and we both ran toward the bedroom dragging a double mattress behind us.

Joy dove on the floor first as the rest of us literally "hit the floor," and accidentally, on top of her. Dad and Jimmy grabbed the mattress off Mom's and Dad's bed and threw it on top of us with the other mattresses, pillows, and blankets we had dragged from the front room.

Together, they pushed furniture against the bedroom wall and selflessly lunged in front of it to act as a barrier for the rest of us. If any bullets came though the wall, the furniture would be hit first, then Dad and Jimmy and then the girls. Dad and Jimmy were doing all they could to stop or slow down the bullets and to protect the girls in the family.

The walls, mattresses, furniture, and pillows

were our only hope of slowing down bullets if they came through the window or wall or if the soldiers burst into the apartment.

Our arms and legs crisscrossed one another. We didn't care. We were doing what we could to be safe. We tried not to breathe out loud lest we be heard and discovered. No one dared whisper for fear that we'd be heard.

We hoped we looked like a pile of old mattresses and dirty laundry. I can only imagine how we must have looked trying to protect our lives.

We all touched someone nearby to protect us or for protection as we waited breathlessly for the shooting to stop.

After what seemed like forever the gunfire finally stopped. Whispering, Mom told us to say our names in our birth order to be sure we were all there and safe.

The first voice whispered, "Mary," then — too long of a silence. We panicked and remembered Ruthie was safe in the states. Almost in unison we breathed a sigh of relief. We continued. Francie, Gale, Jimmy, Debbie and then it was Joy's turn.

Silence. There was no reply.

"Joy?" we whispered. Where was she? What happened? We were frightened and someone started to cry. Then we heard a tiny voice say, "I'm here. I can't breathe! You are all on top of me and Mary's curler is in my eye!"

We were so relieved! We quickly moved and adjusted our positions under the mattresses to give her room. For the moment we were all safe and silently thanked God.

Throughout the night, sporadic gunfire continued. Each time it began, we were afraid someone was aware of our family hiding under mattresses in the two-room apartment.

The gunfire overhead began a night of sleeping under mattresses, instead of on top of them as we had done our entire lives. It was our only protection.

As we tried to go to sleep Debbie said, "If it's our time to die, it's our time to die" We all silently agreed. We had been raised with a strong faith in Jesus Christ.

And then Dad began to snore. For a moment, Dad relaxed but his snoring scared us! We were afraid someone might hear it and come into the apartment. Later that night, a cat began to howl. It sounded like it was in the courtyard.

Hearing the cat, Joy began to cry because she was worried about and fearful for the cat. Others started to cry too, as softly as possible, because they were scared, and no one wanted to be heard by the invading soldiers outside. We had just lived through a harrowing experience and had no idea what the next minute would bring. Then Jimmy said, "Does anybody have an apple?" His tired and true ridiculous told-too-many-times joke brought us moments of relief.

Someone realized they had to go to the bathroom, down the hall. That started a chain reaction among us all. It was after midnight. It was dark. After hearing and seeing the bullets overhead for what seemed forever, the silence was nearly deafening.

Joy quietly and slowly crawled out from under everyone and the mattress. Debbie quickly joined her. I followed. We all tiptoed to the bathroom we shared with the other boarders.

As quietly as possible, Joy and Debbie walked down the hall. Joy saw a door that opened onto another room. She looked inside the room and saw a man lying on the bed. His head was wrapped in a blood-soaked cloth; He was bleeding from a gunshot wound. A woman was sitting beside him, whispering to him, as she held a rag to his head to try to stop the bleeding. The woman's back was to the open door. She turned and saw Joy looking at the injured man. Without hesitation and a steady gaze into Joy's eyes, the woman got up, and quickly, shut the door.

We got to the bathroom and saw a bloody rag and blood on the sink. Someone had been shot.

CHAPTER SIX

Back in the United States, Ruthie was at work when she heard the news Czechoslovakia had been invaded. She had left us just before we entered the country and, not knowing our travel schedule, had no idea if we were in Czechoslovakia. She didn't know what to do or think and was worried sick. All of this while beginning a new teaching job and trying to prepare and focus her attention on her students.

Thoughts swirled in her mind. Was her family dead or alive? Would she ever see us again? She was forced to push the thoughts from her mind, so she could concentrate on her students and wait for some kind of communication from us if one were to come.

Twenty-four-hour news cycles, cell phones, the internet and social media did not exist in 1968. The only way to communicate was by mail, airmail or, if available, by expensive long-distance phone call.

Then a strange thing happened when, for no apparent reason, Ruthie was called to the principal's office. She was nervous and gravely concerned. Upon entering the office, the principal gave Ruthie a note from the Red Cross. The note simply stated, "Your family is in Czechoslovakia. They are alive." That was it. No other information. To this day I don't know how the Red Cross knew about us and found Ruthie and the school where she was teaching.

CHAPTER SEVEN

The next day, Dad bravely continued to walk the streets of Prague as he calmly sought a way to get us out of the country and safely home. As he came and went, he would take one or two of us into Wenceslas Square to show and teach us, firsthand, the horrors of war. He wanted us to remember and never forget. Eventually, he let us go without him if we were with a sibling.

When it was my turn Dad took me down the dark stairwell through the protective courtyard, into the main street to see and remember the stark reality of face-to-face war. At first glance of the capitol city block, I was momentarily reminded of glamorous, unrealistic war movies. But this was not on the screen. It was real. Tanks lined both sides of the street, end-to-end. Soldiers marched relentlessly with their eyes darting, guns slung over their shoulders, with another held in their hand.

Hunks of metal which resembled stacked, flattened old garbage cans were carelessly shoved on the sidewalks, in the median and on the street. Upon a second glance the resemblance ceased, and the harsh realization set in these garbage cans had once been automobiles which heavy tanks has simply "rolled over," and destroyed.

It was in Wenceslas Square where we saw the enormous tanks with their massive guns lining the streets, pointing those guns at everything in sight - including us. Where we witnessed the shouting protests of thousands of people led by those carrying a blood-soaked Czechoslovakian flag; where we saw the flattened cars, bikes, and motorbikes that had taken decades for their owners to buy, and the huge buses shoved aside like toys. People began giving us slips of paper and letters to take out of the country, (*if* we got out of the country) to send to their relatives. We soundlessly prayed for the citizens holding their country's flag as they repeatedly shouted, "Dubček! Svoboda! Dubček! Svoboda!" Dubček, the name of their party leader and Svoboda, the name if their President. Svoboda also means freedom.

We heard random gunfire as the soldiers shot up the National Museum of Prague, office buildings, shops, and everything else in their sight. Every time the gunfire began, we ran into the Hotel Europa (Evropa) for cover and hid until the gunfire ceased.

My sister Mary, a local radio and television personality back home, was the first one to go into the Square with Dad. Dads' instinct told him someone would need to know what was happening in Prague, so at great risk, the two of them gathered as much information as possible and secretly took photographs and recorded interviews.

Wearing her trench coat, Mary taped interviews with locals using the recorder she had just purchased during our trip to use for her work at home. She hung the recorder over her shoulder and hid it under her trench coat. She ran the mic wire down her sleeve and cupped the mic in the palm of her hand. In this way she was able to talk to and record interviews with those living through this horrific experience.

There was a time when most of us were in the Square. Debbie and I stuck together and eventually returned to the apartment. As we began walking up the dark stairwell to the third floor, we saw that the military had taken over the telegraph office building a few feet from our apartment. What had once been exciting was now frightening. The armed soldiers were guarding each floor along the outdoor corridors of the telegraph building as they slowly walked from end to end.

In the dark stairwell, Debbie and I flattened ourselves against the wall, desperately trying not to attract attention or be seen by the soldiers as we slowly climbed the stairs. The sound of gunfire from the Square, ringing in our ears.

Reaching the top floor, we ran into the apartment and saw Mom and Joy standing like statues in the middle of the room. Their expressions quickly went from anxious worry to relief. They told us while we were out, they heard a single gunshot followed by a second shot and silence. When the third shot rang out, they started counting each time they heard a gun fire. There were several minutes between each shot as the slow gunfire continued. Four, five, six, seven and then — complete silence.

They held onto each other and began to ask questions: Had the family been shot? Were they dead or alive? Were Mom and Joy the only family members left? They didn't know the answers until Debbie, and I ran into the apartment. At least two of us were safe. One by one the rest of the family entered the apartment. All accounted for and safe!

With our passports, Dad constantly went to Hotel Europa to continue his search for a way home and how to get in touch with the American Embassy. It had become the unofficial headquarters for foreigners and residents caught in the invasion, including scientists attending the International Convention of Archeologists.

Day-after-day they all worked to find a way out and decided to try to leave the country by auto convoy. They invited our family to join them!

The convoy was to leave early the next morning. It was to meet with others from around the country in the town of Plzeň about one hundred kilometers away. Dad was encouraged. He felt he had found a way to get us across the border and home.

He came bursting into the apartment, told us to pack up because we were leaving early the next morning. We immediately started packing. We were lucky. We still had the Truckey Bus. It had not been crushed by the Russian tanks because, on a strange instinct, the night before the invasion, Dad had parked it in a garage.

CHAPTER EIGHT

Early the next morning, our family must have set a world record as we finished packing our suitcases and desperately threw our belongings together. The sun was our only light, as we made multiple trips, practically running, down three flights of the dark stairwell, to the Truckey Bus. We accidentally drew attention to ourselves loading the bus. We passed armed soldiers in the courtyard who didn't take their eyes off us and watched as we packed the bus.

Tears streamed down the faces of the Czech citizens. Without us asking, they begin carrying and helping us load our luggage. People secretly passed us post cards to mail if we crossed the border into freedom. The correspondence was hidden in our clothing for fear of confiscation.

Debbie and Francie used their perfected, organized system to rapidly pack our bags in the luggage rack on the top of Truckey Bus. When finished, Debbie jumped off the top of the bus and we were ready to go but not before hugs and kisses were exchanged with those who helped us pack and who we were helpless to help.

As the last person to leave the apartment, I quickly made my way down the stairs to the bus. I nearly collided with an armed soldier, holding a rifle across his chest. He blocked my path. We stopped on the dark landing and looked at one another for what seemed like an eternity. I held my breath.

Thoughts raced through my mind. Would he shoot or arrest me? Would he let me pass? Should I run by him? What should I do? I waited. We stared at each other and, finally, he shoved past me and ran up the stairs. I was momentarily stunned and then ran down the stairs to the street, jumped into the Truckey Bus and we took off.

I will always remember his face and his piercing, dark eyes. I will never stop wondering who or what he sought on the top floor.

We begin our journey to Plzeň to join the convoy. We had to cross over Charles Bridge and the river Vltava. But the bridge was blocked by several armed tanks and soldiers. In the broken Czechoslovakian language from his childhood, Dad leaned to the passenger window and asked the soldiers to let us cross. They ignored him. We drove on looking for another bridge to cross, but each bridge was blocked, and Dad was ignored.

A local man witnessed our plight and flagged us over. In broken English and hand gestures, he told us he lived on the other side of the river and was trying to get home. He said he thought he could get us out of the city if he could ride with us and translate. Dad told him to get on the bus. We shifted our seats to give him room. He jumped in the front seat with Mom and Dad. We prayed his plan would work. He was our second miracle in a vast sea of people in Prague.

We drove to the next bridge, and, with his help, we were blocked again. Determined to find a way we drove on looking for another bridge. We found it, and he convinced the soldiers to let us cross. Once on the other side, he got out of the bus, and we were on our way to Plzeň. We never saw him again.

Due to all the blocked bridges, we were off time and track to Plzeň and needed to find our way to the town. We used a paper map and road signs to figure out where to go because superhighways and GPS did not exist. On the small, two-lane roadways, we headed for Plzeň, a determined expression on Dad's face. He was focused on getting his family to safety, but it still seemed so far out of reach.

As we drove through town after town, our car was the only car on the road. After a while we began to see other cars and realized that we were all moving in the same direction. The small group of cars grew larger and larger and formed an unofficial convoy headed for Plzeň and the border.

As we drove, we discovered road after road was blocked with at least three fully armed tanks. Each surrounded by soldiers pointing their guns at us, almost daring us to try to drive by. *En masse* the growing convoy would turn around to search for another road to Plzeň. We drove through countless towns. In each town, hundreds of people lined the streets, scared and sobbing because their homeland had been invaded. They had become prisoners in their own homes but cheered us on as we drove by. They waved the

Czechoslovakian flag in support of their leaders and yelled "Please help us! Please tell the world what is really happening here."

They handed us small Czechoslovakian flags through our bus windows. We waved the flags in support of the people. As in the Square, people handed us letters to mail and phone numbers to call friends and relatives *if* we got out of the country.

Everywhere we looked, there were signs painted in support of Dubček and Svoboda. Signs were painted on the streets, on sheets hanging from windows and on pieces of cardboard. Huge black drapes hung on the sides of buildings. Using the paint, we had used to label our luggage we painted "Dubček" and "Svoboda" on our suitcases.

I was astounded at the number of painted signs. Leaning on the front seat of the Truckey Bus, I said to no one in particular, "Why don't they use guns? Paint brushes are the only weapons they have to fight with." It was a simple and profound observation.

Dad told us the Czechoslovakian people didn't have guns for their personal protection, so they couldn't fight the Warsaw Pact alone or in groups. They didn't have guns because the guns had been registered with the government and were instantly taken away when the Russians invaded.

With great courage and determination, the Czechoslovakian people fought bravely by yelling, protesting, throwing rocks at the soldiers and tanks. They waved flags and painted multiple signs in all sizes, on any surface they could find.

In our enthusiastic support we continued to wave the Czech flags out of the Truckey Bus windows. Occasionally, due to traffic, the convoy stopped. At one stop, the driver of another car came up to Dad's window and told him the cars in the convoy were dropping far behind us, fearing that we might be targeted. They said we should stop waving the Czech flags for everyone's safety.

CHAPTER NINE

It was midday when the convoy entered another town and unexpectedly stopped. Once again, tanks and soldiers blocked us. But instead of turning around, Dad and several other drivers in the convoy decided to stop and wait to see what would happen. Instantly, questions filled our minds: Would this be the end of our journey to freedom? Would we be forced to give up?

Dad got out of the Truckey bus and spoke to other drivers. Together they discovered many of the cars were nearly out of gas, so helped one another by siphoning gas from each other's cars using found materials. I remember watching Dad siphoning gas from the Truckey Bus into a container for another car. For hours we solemnly waited while whispering and hoping that our long, frightening journey to freedom would continue.

Our Truckey Bus was close to the front of the convoy. The soldiers' voices drifted to our ears. We intently watched the huge tanks that blocked the road, surrounded by soldiers with their rifles and guns. It was impressive, frightening, daunting and surreal.

Inside the bus we spoke in hushed tones. Several times, Dad got out of the bus to speak to others in the convoy and to the townspeople. With tears running down their cheeks they repeatedly said, "Please help us."

In an impulse we started giving the towns people our personal items. Mary gave her gold bracelets and Jimmy gave a young boy the expensive watch he had just purchased during our trip. The young boys' face lit up in disbelief. Immediately he turned to the crowd to show the gift the American boy gave him.

CHAPTER TEN

No one had any idea what would happen and when. Whispers spread up and down the convoy. We were trapped because the armed soldiers and tanks would not let us pass. Without warning we had become prisoners in our own cars!

A black limousine came up the dusty road and passed by us with its country's flags flying from its hood. Its driver drove up to the tanks and stopped. A well-dressed dignitary got out and confidently walked to the soldiers and the tanks.

He spoke to the soldiers and told them to move and to let the cars pass. The soldiers just looked at him and said "Ne," (No). They pointed their guns at the dignitary and told him to get back into his car.

A second limousine drove up the road and to the tanks. Its country's flag attached to the corner of its hood. The dignitary got out of his car. He spoke to the soldiers and told them to move. The soldiers pointed their guns directly at the dignitary and told him to get back in the car.

A third limousine drove up to the enormous tanks with its country's flags flying. The dignitary got out of his car and the same thing happened as before.

No one knew what to do, including the dignitaries, who stood with each other trying to work out a solution. Everyone was concerned. Many were scared. Some were afraid that they were going to die in their car while waiting to drive past the tanks and get to Plzeň and then to the border.

The soldiers would not budge for any of the nations. Was it hopeless? Would we get out of Czechoslovakia and home to America? Would the others in the convoy get back to their homelands?

Dark clouds covered the sky and hung over the convoy like a heavy gray blanket. The sun seemed to watch from behind the clouds waiting to see our fate. Only time would tell.

CHAPTER ELEVEN

Then it happened.

A large station wagon bearing a huge flag on its roof and its country's representatives inside, drove to the tanks and confronted the Soviet military. The flag consisted of a brilliant blue background with white stars and deep red and white stripes. It was the American flag!

We were thrilled to see our flag but did not know what would happen. Three countries had tried to get through but to no avail. Would the soldiers listen to the dignitary from the United States and let us through? Or would we once again be told to stay where we were?

We silently watched and waited, wide-eyed and praying, as we held our collective breath.

The representatives got out of the car and walked to the soldiers and tanks. He spoke to the soldiers. They spoke back. Time stood still.

There were fierce negotiations to allow the international convoy to pass the blockade. The silence was intense except for the voice of the Russians in command and the Americans.

Much to our shock, one by one, the soldiers started lowering their guns and slowly got into the tanks. We didn't know if they were going to move the tanks or drive over and shoot us all. We didn't say a word as we watched the suspenseful moments unfold before our eyes. Our lives changed again.

Suddenly, a thundering sound and the roar of the tank's engines filled the air. The tanks slowly began to move to the side of the road. We could not believe it! Quiet cheers went up and many began to cry in gratitude. Our family was proud to belong to the beautiful flag and the country it represented.

One at a time the sound of car engines starting was heard up and down the line of cars. Tentatively, the convoy began to crawl as it crept by the tanks. Everyone kept their eyes mostly straight ahead with tiny darting glances at the soldiers and tanks on the side of the road. And at that moment I knew. . .

CHAPTER TWELVE

. . . I realized and understood how powerful and respected America is to the world. That's when I understood why Mom and Dad raised the American flag every day, and on national holidays we all said,

> *"I pledge allegiance to the flag*
> *of the United States of America*
> *and to the Republic for which it stands, one Nation under God, indivisible, with liberty and justice for all."*

That is why we sang patriotic songs and at times talked about America's history, said a prayer thanking God for our great nation and asked Him to bless America.

My parents were working to instill in us a life-long respect, appreciation and love for our country, the United States of America, a true Republic. It was an undying love they both shared.

CHAPTER THIRTEEN

Bit by bit the convoy moved. Our journey proceeded beyond Plzeň to the Czechoslovakian and German border.

Reaching the boarder passports were collected, cars were searched, and cameras were confiscated. Because of our Czechoslovakian name, Nemec, (Nimitz) a common Czechoslovakian name, the border guards thought we were citizens attempting to illegally leave the country.

We were frustrated at seeing a free allied country less than one hundred yards away. We watched numerous cars pass and go before us, as Dad worked to convince the authorities we were American citizens going home and not Czechoslovakian's attempting to defect. Instead of proceeding, our family was held at the border for hours and our lives changed again.

It was hot. We had no food or water. For more than eight hours countless cars passed by us, allowed to leave the country. Armed soldiers would approach and search the Truckey Bus again and again. They would look in the bus and say, "Nemitz!" Francie, stating the American pronunciation, would determinedly say, "Knee-mick." We all followed her lead, and loudly repeated "Knee-mick." The soldiers wanted to take items out of the bus, but Dad would not let them. He said he would destroy our things rather than let them be confiscated.

While we were waiting, a crowded, green bus drove

up to the border and came to a halt. Its windows were open as in those days there was no air conditioning on buses. We looked up at the bus and, in a passenger seat by the window, sat Ambassador Shirley Temple Black. We were so excited! Shirley Temple Black was on the bus! We had two books with us on the trip: The Holy Bible and the children's story book written by Ambassador Black. We had been reading both books.

Joy and Debbie jumped out of the Truckey Bus with Joy clutching the storybook. I ran behind them. Debbie lifted Joy to the open window and handed the book to the Ambassador. Ambassador Black closed her eyes and hugged it to her chest. When she opened her eyes, they were filled with tears. She signed the book and gave it back to Joy. A few minutes later her bus left, and our long wait continued.

Again, a soldier came to search the Truckey Bus, feeling under the seats, rifling through papers, and tossing bags. Slowly, he looked each of us in the eye and then he looked at Mary who was seated in the back seat of the Truckey Bus. We all knew that she was hiding most of the rolls of film, recorded tapes, letters, and phone numbers in her undergarments. We did not want to think what would happen if she or if any of us were caught.

Suddenly we all heard yelling and gunfire and saw a Czechoslovakian soldier running to escape into Germany. He ran down a ravine and was chased by several Russian soldiers. The soldier searching our bus lost interest in us. He ran after the others who shot and caught the escaping soldier and forcefully dragged him back to the newly occupied country of Czechoslovakia. We continued to wait at the border.

Countless times Dad went between our bus and the border office, calmly using his verbal skills and our passports as he worked to convince the guards we were American citizens and to let us cross the border. Each time he got back on the bus he and Mom would speak with each other so softly we could hardly hear them. We wondered what they were saying.

It was dusk, and the sun was going down. It had been a long day. We had been on the bus, working our way out of the country since the early, early morning.

We had been at the border for hours when I suddenly realized Dad had been out of the bus and was returning quickly and calmly with a focused look on his face. He slid behind the wheel and started the engine. I asked him if we were leaving. He looked straight ahead and whispered to Mom. I stopped asking questions. The engine came to life. I wished the engine were silent so no one would notice us. The Truckey Bus slowly began to move. No one said a word. As we headed toward the border and its crossing gates. The gates went up and we slowly drove through.

When I thought we had crossed the border, as quietly as I could I started asking, "Have we crossed? Have we crossed? Have we crossed the border?" My voice got a bit louder. Dad, looking straight ahead, softly said, "Yes" with a slight nod to his head.

When I knew we had crossed the border I threw open the sliding door of the Truckey Bus and jumped out. The bus was still moving slowly. Somebody called after me. Debbie and Joy followed. I was so grateful we were safely out of Czechoslovakia that I kissed the paved road twice. Debbie did, too.

The pavement was rough. I did not care. I ran to the first soldier I saw, and I hugged him. Debbie did, too. The shock and surprise on his face when I threw my arms around his belly is engrained in my mind. He was speechless and smiled. Holding his rifle in one hand he put his arm around my back and gave me a hug. I was thrilled and exceedingly grateful that we were free. We could not believe it! We were safe. We had made it safely to Germany.

Unknown to us, a news crew had been filming events taking place at the border. That night Ruthie turned on the television to watch the Huntly Brinkley Report and to find out more about the invasion.

Ambassador Black came on the screen and Ruthie saw Debbie, Jimmy, and me standing with her. Part of our family was on the broadcast! She had no idea where we were, but for the first time since the invasion began, she had solid proof that some of us were still alive. She was so relieved but still worried because she didn't know if we would get out alive, or if we would live to hug and love each other again.

The moment she saw us on television she was overwhelmed with relief and started screaming excitedly. But no one was there to hear her.

Dad's courage, tenacity, determination, leadership, and Navy training, during WWII, got all eight of us out of the war-torn country of Czechoslovakia. Without a GPS, a cell phone, or a tablet, Dad used the problem-solving skills and the magnificent mind that God gave him.

Dad was a rock and our strength. Based on their faith, Dad and Mom were a steady, calming force which kept *us* calm. Even though they may have been experiencing inner turmoil they showed us no fear.

It gave us the quiet assurance that we would be safe, and we would get out. With their faith, Dad's skills, and Mom's confidence in Dad, whatever it took, we would get out and we would get out alive.

Getting out of Czechoslovakia in August 1968, during what came to be known as "Prague Spring," was another one of the miracles experienced by our family.

Later in the car I asked, "Dad, the people of Czechoslovakia can leave this communist country and go to the safety and freedom of America, but if America is ever invaded, where would we go?"

He was silent.

Always remember Prague Spring.

CHAPTER FOURTEEN

According to Soviet Forces, the occupation was to be a temporary one and was to last only until the situation in Czechoslovakia had "normalized." By Soviet standards, the invasion violated one of their own principles, that of sovereignty of all European states and the non-intervention of internal affairs. Czechoslovakia was "temporarily occupied" for more than forty years.

Caught in the crosshairs of war, witnessing firsthand one nation taking over another, seeing soldiers lower their guns, and move their tanks when faced with the American dignitary and the country he represented, are a few of the reasons I fly the American flag outside of my home every day. On national holidays and even when alone, I stand on my porch say the Pledge of Allegiance, sing a patriotic song or two and talk, think or read about America's fascinating and intriguing history. I am grateful to share a bit of history with friends and in my newsletter.

America is a wonderful nation! We have been blessed with hard-working, industrious, self-sufficient citizens who, because they live in the United States of America, have freedoms that allow them to prosper as individuals or groups, regardless of the family they were born into or the state or country where they were born.

We have freedoms and opportunities that hundreds of nations and millions of people have never had; May never have or ever experience in their lifetime. This is why many people come to

America. For freedom, for the freedom to live their lives, to work hard and prosper.

There are countless stories of people who were born here or immigrated here with nothing. They worked hard, studied, listened, learned, pursued an education, or/and an idea. They had a strong work ethic, were constructive and became highly productive citizens who helped to make America a wonderful and unique nation. My father and mother were two of them.

Despite the danger, Dad was right to take us into Wenceslas Square during the invasion. He wanted us to remember what happened and more than 50 years later - I still do.

I will always remember what happened to our family in August 1968, in Czechoslovakia, during Prague Spring. The memories will continue to give me a deep appreciation and love for the United States of America and for the rights granted to us in our Bill of Rights and in the United States Constitution.

If you were born here or are an immigrant who has chosen to become an American citizen or are an immigrant living here, please learn English. The language of our, *now your*, country. The country where *you have chosen to live*. Please read the Constitution of the United States and the Bill of Rights. Brilliant documents that govern us all. It will take you about fifteen minutes to read, daily living to appreciate, and great gratitude and understanding your new nation, its history, and its powerful influence around the world.

Please raise your American flag every day or at the least on National Holidays. Say the Pledge of Allegiance to America, sing America's patriotic songs, learn, and talk about our outstanding history.

Thank God for the freedoms you have because you live in the United States of America. This country is yours, mine, and our HERITAGE.

SPECIAL EDITION   NOVEMBER 24,2024

Nemec Family Capri, Italy
Early August 1968
Copyright 1968-2025 All Rights Reserved

As is evidenced by the above Christmas card, we made it safely home. Dad and Mom used this photo for our 1968 Christmas card. Joy recently found it, took a picture, and texted it to all of us. Immediately, for some of us, it brought memories to light.

Ruthie and Debbie recalled when and where the photo was taken and shared their memories with us.

Ruthie, "I clearly remember the family taking the picture. It was taken near the dock where a ferry left to go to Sicily.

We were in Italy, and on the spur of the moment, Dad thought it would be a good opportunity to visit Sicily since we were close to the ferry. However, because we didn't know the departure schedule, we missed the ferry. In typical Nemec fashion, we lined up near the dock where the ferry had just left and took a picture which we used as our family Christmas card. Instead of going from the toe of Italy at Massina to Sicily we drove over to the "boot heel" of Italy, catching the ferry from Brindisi to Greece. By the way, the ferry's crew was on strike in Brindisi. We had to wait a few days for the strike to end before we could continue our trip.

From Brindisi, we sailed on the Adriatic Sea, and I thought it was wonderful to get to be on a body of water I had only read about. When we got to Greece, one of our stops was in Corinth. Remembering my Sunday School lessons, I started telling the family about the Biblical stories of the "Wicked City of Corinth." I said the word, "prostitutes" and I got in so much trouble from Dad. It was a bad word we were not allowed to say. But the rest of the family came to my rescue and defended me!

Debbie, "I remember having the photo taken and I remember who took it. Do you?" She asked us and none of us could remember. Debbie recalled that the sisters saw three American men, smiled and as usual, struck up a conversation. We learned they were soldiers on military leave. The conversation progressed and we became friendly; so, Dad asked them to take our pictures. After a bit we discovered we were all headed to the same town. Dad and the boys decided to drive in tandem and it was a blessing that we did.

Somewhere along the way our Truckey Bus broke down. Luckly the soldiers were following us and along with Dad, worked into the night to fix whatever the problem was. We were on the side of the road so in the meantime, Mom pulled out blankets for us to sit on and snacks to tie our tummies over till dinner.

Dad and the boys took turns holding the flashlight and studying the engine and also shimmed under the bus to study the engine from below. Ruthie pulled out her guitar and we sang until the bus was repaired.

I remember thinking at the time how nice it was of these Marines to stay with us until the bus was repaired.

As it got darker with cars whizzing by, I also remember what a secure feeling I had that these strong, brave men were with us in case we had any other kind of trouble.

Before we parted ways, they said it was so nice to run into Americans because it reminded them of home.

Dad and Mom taught us to respect the USA and those who were in the military. So, it was natural for us to tell the boys how much we appreciated their Military service. It meant so much to them!

Our family in the 1960's. Easter Sunday. Copyright 1960-2025.

A FEW OF OUR NATION'S HOLIDAYS

Read and learn about our national holidays and celebrate America, your homeland!

Independence Day-The Fourth of July
Thanksgiving
Veterans Day
Presidents Day
Pearl Harbor Day
Martin Luther King Jr. Day
Memorial Day
Flag Day

A FEW PATRIOTIC SONGS
The Star-Spangled Banner
This Land is Your Land
You're a Grand 'Ole Flag
This is My Country
My Country 'Tis of Thee
A Salute to Patriots

ON NATIONAL HOLIDAYS YOU CAN...
. . .raise your American flag.
. . .say the Pledge of Allegiance
. . .sing Patriotic songs.
. . . read and think about our history.
. . .say a prayer of thanks.
. . . ask God to Bless America
. . . read! Talk about the United States Constitution
. . .write a song, poem, or story about *What America Means to Me*.
Email it to: GaleNemecBooks@gmail.com

ABOUT THE AUTHOR

Gale Nemec is an award-winning producer, actress, voice talent. She is also a print model and song writer and writes Christian and children's books, some of which she illustrated, all of which are educational in some capacity. She created and produced *The Bea & the Bug* an award winning, multimedia, interactive, live musical show which features American History. She is currently working on a spin off new series, *Adventures in Time,* an upbeat web series about America's history. Gale wrote and produced Your Song the Ten Commandments Song now on Gale Nemec's YouTube channel and Vimeo.com Gale Nemec. She would love to hear your story, song, or poem about why you love America and may include your story in her next book, on her website www.GaleNemecBooks.com or on her Facebook page Gale Nemec Books.

ABOUT THE ILLUSTRATOR

John Fristoe Sr. (Ret.) A few months ago, John discovered he could draw and that he could draw in pen and ink. With that discovery he started taking art classes and drawing landscapes. This is the first time he has illustrated a book and its cover.

FRONT COVER ARTIST

Facebook: Dawn LeGros
Sharing Is Caring eBook Covers by Dawn - eBook and book cover designs (wordpress.com)

BACK COVER PHOTO

Betsy Royall Casting and Photography Baltimore MD
Betsy Royall Casting and Photography

BOOKS, E-BOOKS, AUDIO BOOKS
BY GALE NEMEC
Ask your local bookstore for Gale's books!
Visit www.GaleNemecBooks.com

Little Stockey & The Miracle of Christmas
There's A Bear on A Bench
The Great Elephant Rescue
Throwing Rocks in the River
Trevor and the T's
Hugging God
Hugging Jesus
Valentine Cards for the Christian Faith
Valentine Cards for Valentine's Day
Dragon in the Mirror, a rhyming coloring book
A Window into Heaven
Hugs, Two a memory photo book
Andy's Adventurous Nightmare
A Wish for You
Santa's Gift
God Held Your Hand

SPANISH & BILINGUAL BOOKS
Hay un Oso En La Banca (There's A Bear on a Bench)
El Pequeño Stockey y el Milagro de la Navidad (Little Stockey & the Miracle of Christmas)

NON-FICTION
Caught in the Crosshairs of War

GALE READING HER BOOKS ON YOU TUBE (Interactive)
There's a Bear on a Bench
Throwing Rocks in the River

FAMILY VIDEOS AVAILABLE ONLINE
Live! Little Stockey &
the Miracle of Christmas

More books on the way! Thank you for buying, reading, or giving this book as a gift. Look up Gale Nemec on *Good Reads, Amazon* and more. Please subscribe to my YouTube channel Gale Nemec. Please rate this book with a review or a star value. Thank you!

www.ingramcontent.com/pod-product-compliance
Lightning Source LLC
Chambersburg PA
CBHW072016060426
42446CB00043B/2598